Dig it

Written by Leilani Sparrow
Photographed by Will Amlot

Collins

Dad pats the dog.

3

Dad tips a pot.

Dad digs a pit.

7

Dad pats the top.

Pop the tap on.

11

Dad tips it on.

/g/

After reading

Letters and Sounds: Phase 2

Word count: 48

Focus phonemes: /g/ /o/

Common exception words: is, the

Curriculum links: Understanding the World: The World

Early learning goals: Listening and attention: listen attentively in a range of situations; Understanding: Answer 'how' and 'why' questions about experiences and in response to stories or events; Reading: read and understand simple sentences, use phonic knowledge to decode regular words and read them aloud accurately, read some common irregular words

Developing fluency

- Go back and read the chant to your child, using lots of expression.
- Make sure that your child follows as you read.
- Pause so they can join in and read with you.
- Say the whole chant together. You can make up some actions to go with the words.

Dad pats the dog.
It is a map.
Dad tips a pot.
Pop it on top.

Dad digs a pit.
Pop it in, Dad.
Dad pats the top.
Pat the top, Sam.

Pop the tap on.
Tip it on top.
Dad tips it on.
Tip it on top.

Phonic practice

- Say the word **dog**. Ask your child if they can sound out each of the letter sounds in the word **dig** d-i-g and then blend them. Ask them if they can think of any words that rhyme with **dig**. (e.g. *big, fig, gig*)